MAKER MODELS
BIOSPHERE AND MINI-GARDEN

Anna Claybourne

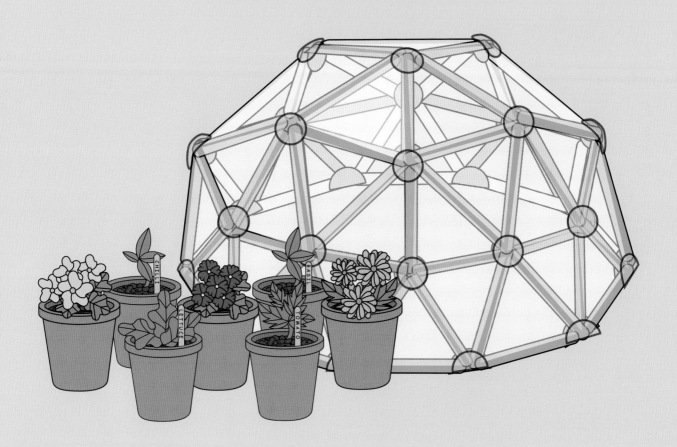

WAYLAND

www.waylandbooks.co.uk

First published in Great Britain in 2019
by Wayland
Copyright © Hodder and Stoughton, 2019

Editor: Elise Short
Design and illustration: Collaborate

HB ISBN 978 1 5263 0745 3
PB ISBN 978 1 5263 0746 0

Printed and bound in China

Wayland, an imprint of
Hachette Children's Group
Part of Hodder and Stoughton
Carmelite House
50 Victoria Embankment
London EC4Y 0DZ

An Hachette UK Company

www.hachette.co.uk
www.hachettechildrens.co.uk

The website addresses (URLs) included in this book were valid at the time of going to press. However, it is possible that contents or addresses may have changed since the publication of this book. No responsibility for uyany such changes can be accepted by either the author or the Publisher.

Note: In preparation of this book, all due care has been exercised with regard to the instructions, activities and techniques depicted. The publishers regret that they can accept no liability for any loss or injury sustained. Always get adult supervision and follow manufacturers' advice when using electric and battery-powered appliances.

CONTENTS

Grow a garden   4
Garden base   6
Grass art   8
Bean tree   10
Wildflower corner   12
Geodesic dome greenhouse   14
Greenhouse garden   18
Fountain   20
Summer house   24
Finishing touches   26

And here is your finished garden!   28

Glossary and further information   30
Index   32

GROW A GARDEN

Gardens come in all shapes and sizes, from tiny window boxes to parks, botanical gardens and ginormous grounds. They add colour to the world with beautiful flowers, and help wildlife by providing food and shelter for insects and birds. People use their gardens to grow fruit and veg, too – or just as a place to relax and play.

If you love growing things and being creative, this book is for you. It shows you how to make your own miniature model garden or biosphere with real plants. The biosphere is everything that is alive on Earth, but a human-made biosphere is a building in which a biome is recreated, such as a rainforest or woodlands.

It could also be a great garden for toy figures – they can sit out on the miniature benches and seats, have a sleepover in the summer house or go for a swim in the fountain.

NO GARDEN? NO PROBLEM!

Of course, not everyone is lucky enough to have their own real garden. If you do have one, you might be able to use a corner of it for your model mini-garden. If not, your garden can also be set up indoors, near a sunny window, in a porch, on a veranda, or on a balcony, as long as there's a bit of space you have permission to use.

MAKER MATERIALS

For the projects in this book, you'll need some basic gardening equipment and materials, such as compost and seeds. You can find these at a garden centre, or at a big supermarket (especially in spring and summer). You don't need lots of expensive stuff, though – for example, old yoghurt pots or ice-cream tubs make good plant pots.

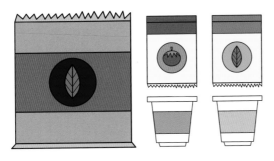

Some projects use household items and craft materials, such as old food containers, glue, modelling clay and lolly sticks or craft sticks. You can find most craft items at a toy store or hobby store. See page 31 for a list of useful sources.

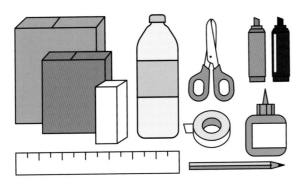

BLOOP BLOOP! SAFETY ALERT!

For some of the projects, you'll need to use sharp tools, such as a craft knife, or an electric appliance like a hot glue gun.

For anything involving sharp objects, heat or electricity, always ask an adult to help and supervise. And make sure you keep items like these in a safe place, away from where younger children could find them.

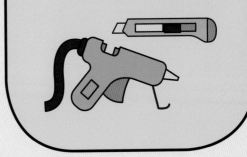

WATCH OUT FOR PETS!

If possible, put your garden somewhere where pets can't go, as they could easily knock over, flatten or mess up your creations. Unfortunately, when dogs and cats see soil, they sometimes like to poo in it! So keep them away if you can.

Charity shops are a great place to look for old, cheap household items and materials, too.

CAN I USE THIS?

Before you start emptying the cupboards, make sure any containers or household items you want to use are finished with, clean and you have permission to use them for your green-fingered creations. Now, you're ready to get gardening!

GARDEN BASE

Your mini-garden needs a space to go in and a base to sit on. If it's outdoors, it could go on a flat area of garden. If it's indoors, or on a balcony or veranda, it needs some kind of tray or container. Here are three options. Choose the one that works best for you.

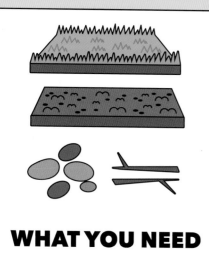

WHAT YOU NEED

- A small area of garden lawn or bare soil
- Pebbles or sticks

Option 1: Outdoor space

Best if: you have an outdoor area of grassy ground or soil. (Remember this garden will get rained on, so some of your models might not last as long as they would indoors.)

1 If possible, choose a sunny location in a corner or next to a wall or fence, as it will be less windy. Make sure you have permission to use the space.

2 Your garden can be any shape. You can make it bigger or smaller, but a good size is about 70–80 cm square, or a 50 cm by 100 cm rectangle.

3 Use sticks or pebbles to make a boundary around the edge of your garden area, so everyone knows where it is.

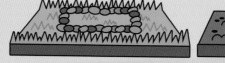 

Option 2: Indoor or outdoor garden tray

Best if: you have an indoor area, or a sheltered outdoor area, such as a covered balcony or veranda with a hard surface.

1 Unless you have one already, you need to buy the tray from a garden centre or order one online, so this isn't the cheapest option. Look for a tray around 70–80 cm square, or 50 cm by 100 cm. It should be hard plastic with no holes.

2 Put the tray in a safe, sunny spot. Pour in a bag of sand, such as play sand from a toy shop, or gardening sand from a garden centre. Spread the sand out evenly.

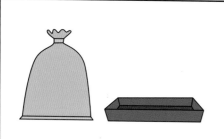

WHAT YOU NEED

- A large garden drip tray or hydroponics tray
- A bag of sand

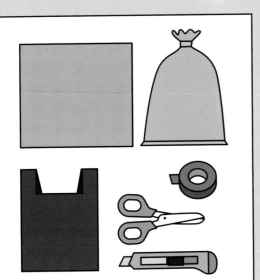

WHAT YOU NEED

- A very large strong cardboard box, or piece of cardboard
- Scissors or craft knife
- A large plastic bin bag or a waterproof garden sack
- Strong sticky tape
- A bag of sand

Option 3: Indoor home-made tray

Best if: you need a tray, as in option 2, but cheaper! This will only work somewhere that won't get any rain on it, as it will get soggy.

1 **Option A:** With an adult's help, cut the sides off a large cardboard box to make a large tray, 8 cm deep. Strengthen any loose parts with sticky tape.

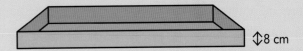

$\updownarrow$8 cm

Option B: If you have flat cardboard, fold the edges up about 8 cm in to make sides. At the corners, cut the card so that the sides can overlap, and tape them together.

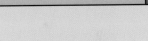

$\updownarrow$8 cm

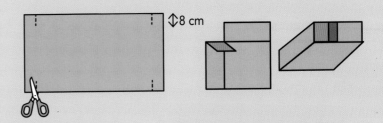

2 Lay the bin bag flat and carefully cut off the base and the handles if there are any. Cut along one side, then open out the plastic into a large sheet.

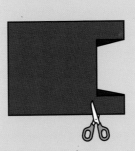

3 Use the plastic to make a waterproof lining for your tray, making sure it fits into all the sides and corners. Fold it over the edges and tape it to the outside of the tray.

TIP

If you have a large, wide windowsill, you could buy or make a tray to fit there – as long as you're sure it won't fall off. (Because that would be extremely messy!)

4 Put the tray in a safe, sunny spot. Pour in a bag of sand, such as play sand from a toy shop or gardening sand from a garden centre. Spread the sand out evenly.

GRASS ART

Don't just grow some grass – make grass art! It could be a letter or word, a shape or symbol, a face, a maze or whatever else you like.

WHAT YOU NEED
- A large, shallow plant container or clean food tray
- A bradawl or thick needle
- An eraser or a cork
- Potting compost
- A small packet of grass seed
- Paper and a pencil
- Scissors
- Kitchen paper
- A large plate
- A fork
- A spray bottle or small watering can (optional)
- Small pebbles or shells (optional)

Look for a 'patch pack' of grass seed, which only contains a small amount and is cheaper.

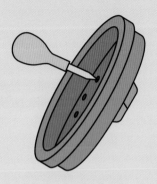

1 Make sure your plant container or food tray has drainage holes. If it doesn't, ask an adult to make some by pushing a bradawl or thick needle through the base a few times, into an eraser or cork on the other side.

2 Turn the container upside down and draw around it on to a piece of paper, to give you the exact size and shape. Draw the design for your grass art inside the shape. It needs to be quite simple and clear – avoid small details, as they won't show up. How about …

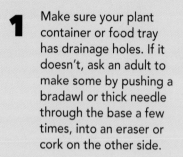

A star

A smiley face

A letter

Draw around your hand

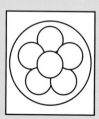

A flower

Make a simple grass maze

3 Put the container into your garden area or tray, so that it can drain on to the ground or the sand. Pour compost into it, then break up and flatten down the compost using a fork. Do this until the container is almost full to the top.

4 Cut out your design. Draw around it on to a piece of kitchen paper. Cut it out carefully. Put the kitchen paper shape (or shapes) on to the plate. Sprinkle or spray it with water until it's soaked. With dry hands, sprinkle grass seed all over it.

5 Carefully pick up the wet, seed-covered kitchen paper (this might be easier with two people) and lay it on the soil in the container. Pick off any grass seeds that have fallen off on to the compost.

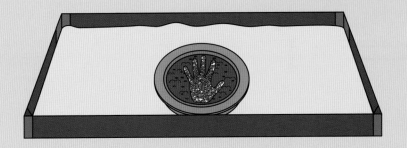

6 Now carefully sprinkle more compost over the shape, so that it's covered in a shallow layer about 1 cm deep. Water the compost gently, with a small watering can or spray bottle if possible. Keep it damp by watering it lightly every day.

7 After week, your grass should start to grow in the shape you made. If you like, you can cover the spaces in between with small pebbles or shells, and trim the grass with scissors if it gets too long.

BEAN TREE

Beans are brilliant plants to have in your garden. They're easy to grow and fast-growing, they have beautiful flowers, and best of all, they give you beans! As your model garden is small, your beans will tower over it like a tree.

WHAT YOU NEED

- A packet of bean seeds (e.g. broad bean, runner bean or French bean)
- A clean, empty glass jar
- Kitchen paper
- Potting compost
- A medium-sized plant pot, or other container, such as an old ice-cream tub
- A bradawl or thick needle
- A spoon
- Three plant sticks, or any long, thin, straight sticks
- An elastic band or string
- A plastic bottle or small yoghurt pot
- Scissors
- A small watering can or spray bottle (optional)

When buying your seeds, look for dwarf varieties or 'dwarf beans' – they are smaller than normal and will suit your garden better.

1 Tear off 2–3 pieces of kitchen paper. Fold them up to make a wad of paper that will fit inside your jar. Push the kitchen paper into the jar so that it is pressed against the sides.

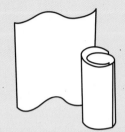

2 Push three bean seeds down between the paper and the glass, spacing them evenly around the jar. Sprinkle or spray the kitchen paper with water until it's soaked through.

3 Put the jar in a warm place, such as a sunny windowsill. Sprinkle or spray it every day to keep the paper damp. In a few days, the bean seeds should start to sprout roots and shoots.

4 If your plant pot or container doesn't have any holes in the bottom, ask an adult to make some by pushing the bradawl or thick needle through the base a few times.

5 Fill the plant pot with compost, pressing it down to make it firm. Make a hole in the middle with the spoon.

6 Choose the seedling that looks strongest and greenest. Gently take it out of the jar and lower the root into the hole in the soil. When the bean is just below the surface, press the compost together around the shoot.

7 Take your three sticks and push them into the compost in a triangle around the edge of the pot. At the top, tie the three sticks together with string or an elastic band.

8 Put a small yoghurt pot, or a small plastic bottle with the top cut off, over the sticks. Don't miss out this step – it stops the sticks from accidentally poking someone in the eye!

9 Put the bean pot in your garden. Water the compost a little every day. The bean plant should grow quite quickly and climb up the sticks. If you're lucky, it will grow flowers, then bean pods with beans inside.

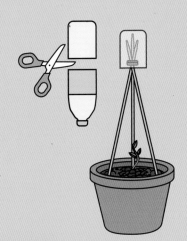

TAKE IT FURTHER ...
You can plant the other beans in pots as well if you like, if you have enough pots and compost.

THE SCIENCE BIT!
Like other plants, bean seeds need water and warmth to germinate or sprout. Once they have leaves, they grow using sunlight, water and carbon dioxide gas from the air – a process called photosynthesis.

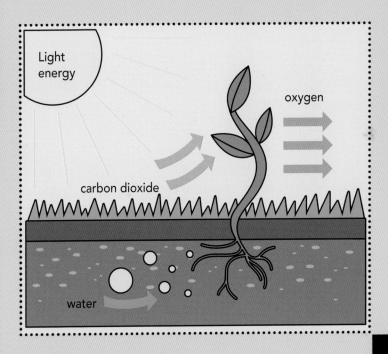

Light energy

oxygen

carbon dioxide

water

WILDFLOWER CORNER

Gardeners often grow exotic flowers that are specially bred for gardens, like fancy varieties of roses, lilies or clematis. Wildflowers are different – they are the flowers that grow naturally in parks, hedgerows and country meadows. And in gardens too, if you give them a chance!

WHAT YOU NEED

- A packet of wildflower seeds
- Gravel or small pebbles
- Larger pebbles or sticks
- Potting compost
- A fork
- A spray bottle or small watering can (optional)

You can buy packets of mixed wildflower seeds at garden centres and supermarkets. However, you may be able to collect some wild seeds too (see pink box on page 13).

1 **Option A:** If your garden is outdoors on an area of grass or soil, you don't need the gravel. Pour potting compost on to a corner or end of your garden, pressing it down and shaping it into a flower bed.

Option B: If your garden is on a tray, in a corner or end of the tray, mark the outline of your flower bed in the sand. Spread a layer of gravel or small pebbles over the sand in this area, this helps the water drain away. Cover it with a deeper layer of compost.

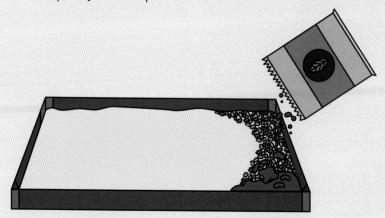

2 Arrange sticks or pebbles along the edge of your flower bed to make a border, which will look nice and also help to hold the compost in place.

3 Gently sprinkle the wildflower seeds evenly over the compost. Then use the fork to rake and turn over the surface, so that the seeds are covered with compost.

4 Gently water the compost with a small watering can or spray bottle, or sprinkle it with water using your fingers. Do this every day to keep the compost damp. The plants should start to grow in a few days.

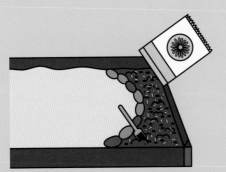

COLLECTING WILD SEEDS

In late summer, wild flowers, such as poppies, clover, buttercups and chicory, make their seeds. If you see any of these plants, you can collect their seeds in a paper bag, and plant them in your garden. Just take a few, so that the plants have some seeds left.

Poppies have little lantern-shaped seed pods. Gently shake the seeds from inside the pod into your bag.

Poppy   Seed pod

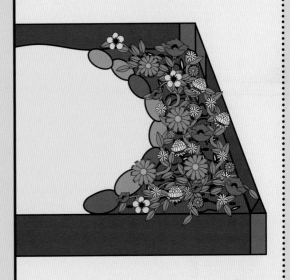

Many flowers develop dry, brownish seed heads, like these. Hold the seed head inside your paper bag, and shake it until some seeds fall off.

Buttercup   Chicory   Clover

Seed head   Seed head   Seed head

THE SCIENCE BIT!

If your garden is outdoors, the wildflowers will provide food and nesting places for bees, butterflies and other wildlife. It's a good idea for all gardens to have a wildflower corner, to help the plants and animals that are local to where you live.

GEODESIC DOME GREENHOUSE

A geodesic dome is a round structure made using a framework of geometric shapes. Domes like this can be used to make tents, houses but they are great for biospheres or greenhouses, as they are strong and provide lots of space.

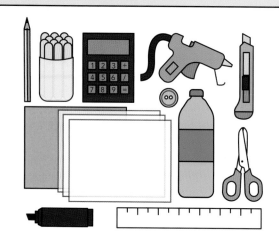

WHAT YOU NEED

- A pack of lolly sticks or thin craft sticks (you will need about 70 of them)
- A calculator
- A ruler and a pencil
- Scissors and a craft knife
- A button or large coin about 2.5 cm wide
- Strong cardboard
- Strong glue or a hot glue gun
- Stiff clear acetate (from a hobby shop or from old acetate packaging)
- A marker pen
- A disposable plastic drinks bottle (optional)

The longer your sticks are, the bigger your greenhouse dome will be. Average-sized lolly sticks, about 11 cm long, will make a dome 35 cm across.

1 First, you need to prepare your sticks, as you will need two different lengths. Take one stick, measure its length and write it down. Using the calculator, divide the number by 7, then multiply the result by 6. Write down the answer.

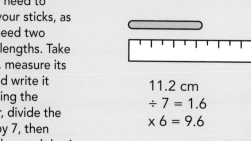

11.2 cm
÷ 7 = 1.6
x 6 = 9.6

2 The result shows how long your shorter sticks need to be. Use the ruler and pencil to mark this length on 30 of your sticks, measuring from one end.

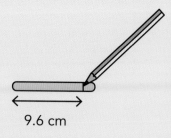

9.6 cm

3 Now cut the sticks off at the marked line. You may be able to do this with strong scissors. Otherwise, ask an adult to use a craft knife to score along the line, then snap the stick neatly.

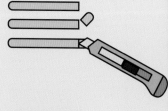

Short sticks

4 Put 30 shorter sticks in a pile and 35 full-length sticks in another pile. In these pictures, we've used different colours to identify the two types of sticks.

Long sticks

5 Draw around your coin or button on to thick card 21 times to make 21 circles. Cut them out. Cut five of them neatly in half to make 10 semicircles.

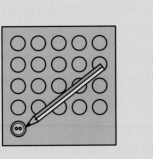 

6 Now you can start building your dome. First, take 10 longer sticks (shown in turquoise) and arrange them into a circular base, like this.

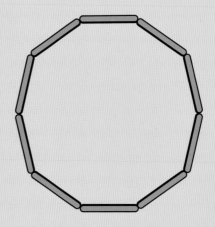

7 Take a cardboard semicircle and glue a stick on to each side of the semicircle to link the sticks together. Do this all the way around the circle. The semicircle should be on the inside of the circle of sticks.

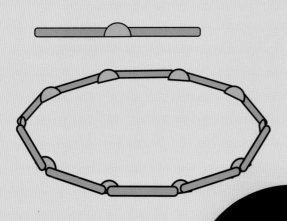

8 Use two more long sticks to make a triangle on top of one of the base sticks. Glue them on to the semicircles at each side of the base stick, and make them meet at the top. Join the sticks by gluing them to a cardboard circle.

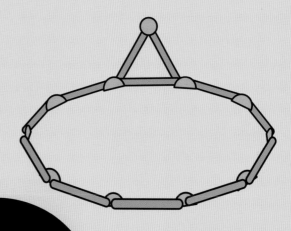

TIP

Make sure you glue the ends of the sticks on to the sides of the cardboard circles, not the middle. This will allow space for all the sticks.

TURN THE PAGE TO CONTINUE ...

9 Make another triangle the same way on the next base stick, but use two of the shorter sticks instead (shown in orange).

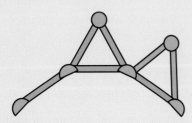

10 Keep working around the circle, alternating the triangles with long sticks and the triangles with short sticks.

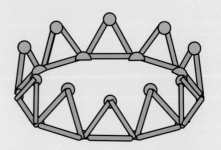

11 Find one of the triangles made with short sticks. Use two more short sticks to connect the top of this triangle to the tops of the triangles on either side with glue.

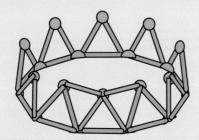

12 Then add a third short stick on the top of the triangle, pointing straight upwards. Repeat steps 11 and 12 with all five of the short triangles around the dome.

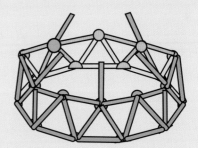

13 Next, use two long sticks, one cardboard circle and glue to connect the upright stick to the sticks on either side. Do this all the way around, so you have five pentagon shapes made from the long sticks.

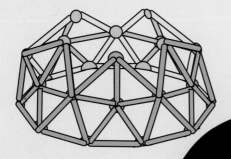

14 Use five long sticks and glue to connect the tops of the pentagons together in a circle. Finally, use five short sticks to make the top of the dome, with one cardboard circle in the middle.

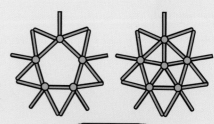

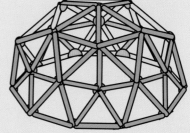

TIP

As you work, you'll find that you have to push the sticks inwards to make them join up, and you will see the dome shape start to appear.

15 Now you can add the greenhouse 'glass'. Take a piece of acetate. Hold it against the dome. Use a marker pen to draw along the sticks to copy the shape of a triangle. Draw the triangle shapes close together on the pieces of acetate so you don't waste any.

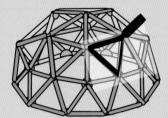

16 Cut out the triangle. Carefully glue its edges on to the sticks to make a window. Repeat steps 15 and 16 for all the other triangles in the dome.

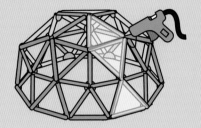

17 This step is optional. Take your coin or button and draw around it with a marker pen on to your plastic drinks bottle 21 times. Cut out the 21 circles with scissors and cut five of them in half.

18 Carefully glue the plastic semicircles and circles in the same places as the cardboard ones, over the tops of the sticks. This isn't essential, but it will make the dome look neater, and help to keep light rain out.

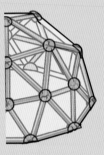

THE SCIENCE BIT!

Greenhouses are used to grow plants that like warm temperatures. As sunlight shines into the greenhouse, it heats up the air and soil inside.
Most of the heat reflects back off the glass and the hot air can't escape, so the temperature inside ends up hotter than outside.

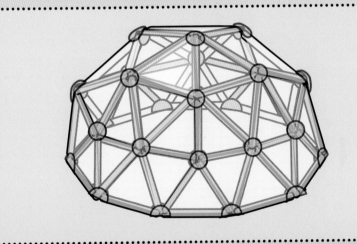

TAKE IT FURTHER ...

If you like making geodesic domes, you could make several of them in different sizes, or try making connected ones.

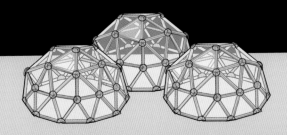

GREENHOUSE GARDEN

Use your geodesic greenhouse to grow some heat-loving vegetable plants, which you can then harvest and eat. To get the best results, whether it's indoors or outdoors, position your greenhouse dome in the sunniest possible spot.

WHAT YOU NEED

- Your geodesic dome greenhouse
- Vegetable seeds or seedlings from a supermarket or garden centre (see box)
- Small plant pots or old yoghurt pots
- Potting compost
- A spoon
- Lolly sticks or strips of cardboard
- A marker pen
- A spray bottle or small watering can (optional)

GREENHOUSE PLANTS

You can either plant your vegetables and flowers from seeds or buy ready-grown seedlings that will grow bigger in your greenhouse. Either way, look for dwarf varieties that should stay nice and small!

Good plants to try are:
- Tomatoes
- Mild chilli peppers
- Lettuce
- Herbs, such as coriander, basil and parsley

1 Decide on a place to put your geodesic greenhouse in your mini-garden. Make sure it's in a place where it will be in full sun for at least some of the day.

2 Arrange your small pots in the space you've picked, then put the dome over them to check they fit. Don't pack them too tightly.

3 Take the dome off again and fill the pots with compost. Press it down firmly with the spoon.

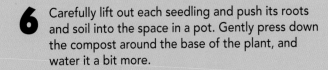

4 If you're using seeds, follow the instructions on the packets that tell you how to plant each type of seed. Plant a few seeds in each pot, then water them until the compost is damp.

5 If you're using seedlings, water them while they are still in their containers, and leave them for a few minutes. Meanwhile, use the spoon to hollow out a space in the compost in each pot.

6 Carefully lift out each seedling and push its roots and soil into the space in a pot. Gently press down the compost around the base of the plant, and water it a bit more.

7 As you do your planting, write the name of each type of plant on a lolly stick or strip of card to make a label. Push it down the side of the plant pot so you know which is which.

8 Put the dome back over the plants. Take it off each day to water the plants and check how they are doing.

TIP

When you have ripe tomatoes or chillis, or salad or herb leaves, you can pick them off. Wash them well before eating!

TAKE IT FURTHER ...

If you don't want to grow vegetables or herbs, you could try some hothouse flowers instead. Flowers that like a nice warm greenhouse include geraniums, nasturtiums, dahlias and marigolds.

FOUNTAIN

All the best gardens have a beautiful, bubbling fountain. The sound of flowing water adds a peaceful atmosphere, and some fountains have fish in them too.

WHAT YOU NEED

- A clear plastic food bowl, such as a salad bowl
- A bradawl or thick needle
- Strong cardboard
- A marker pen and pencil
- Scissors and a craft knife
- Several bendy straws
- Strong glue
- Sticky tape
- A large disposable plastic drinks bottle with a lid
- A small plastic bottle with a spout lid
- Flat, stiff plastic packaging, such as an ice-cream tub lid
- A jug
- Modelling clay or air-drying clay
- A cooking syringe or squeezy bottle
- Paints, paintbrushes and white PVA glue (optional)
- Lots of buttons, beads, sequins or small pebbles (optional)

You can find small bottles with spout lids in most chemists', if you don't have any at home.

1 If you want to paint your fountain, do this first. Mix your paint colour with an equal amount of white PVA glue to make it stick. Paint the outside of your plastic bowl (not the inside, so the water doesn't wash the paint away) and leave it to dry.

2 Make a hole in the middle of the bottom of the plastic bowl, by pushing the bradawl or thick needle through it. Make the hole larger with a pencil, until it is the same width as a straw.

3 Draw around the base of the bowl on to strong card. Cut the circle out and draw a smaller circle in the middle, about 5 cm across. Cut this circle out, then cut a piece out of the side of the circle to make a channel. Your circle will now look like a C shape.

4 Bend the bendy part of the straw at right angles. Push the short end through the hole in the bowl from below. Put strong glue around the straw where it comes through the hole to seal it. Push the longer end of another straw into the top of it, squeezing it slightly to make it fit. Wrap sticky tape around the join.

5 Push the longer end of a third straw into the longer end of the first straw in the same way. Tape them together. Now sit the bowl on to the circle of card, so that the straw lies in the channel. Glue the bowl to the card.

6 With the bradawl or thick needle, make a hole in the side of the large drinks bottle near the base, the same width as a straw. Push the end of the straw into the bottle. Put glue around the hole and then add sticky tape too, to make a tight seal.

7 Take your small spout bottle and make a hole in its base, bigger than the width of a straw. Use strong scissors or a craft knife to cut off the tip of the spout so that a straw can also fit through.

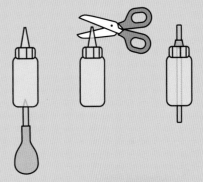

8 Fit the bottle over the straw in the middle of the fountain, so that the straw sticks up out of the spout. Trim the straw off just above the spout.

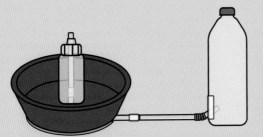

TIP
Avoid using a hot glue gun on plastic bottles and bowls, as they may melt. Use strong craft glue instead.

TURN THE PAGE TO CONTINUE ...

9 Draw a circle on to your flat, stiff plastic packaging, about 10 cm across. Cut it out and make a hole in the middle, slightly larger than the spout on the bottle. Fit the circle over the spout and use a bit of strong glue to hold it in place.

10 When the glue has dried, test your fountain. Ask someone to pinch the straw closed next to the large bottle, while you fill the bottle with water to the top using the jug. Screw the lid on tightly. To make the fountain flow, unscrew the lid. To stop it, put the lid back on.

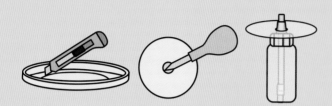

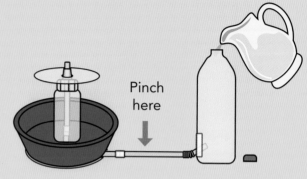

Pinch here

11 To get the water out of the fountain, suck it up using a cooking syringe or squeezy bottle. Squirt it back into the jug to use again.

12 Take out your modelling clay or air-drying clay and roll it into a long, thick rectangle.

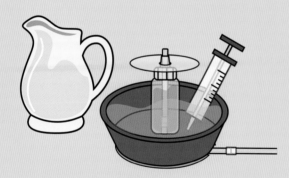

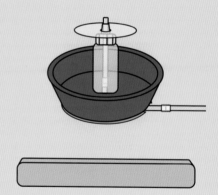

13 Wrap the clay around the bowl to make a wall around the fountain, slightly overlapping the bowl around the top edge. Smooth the clay where it joins together and shape it the way you want – it could be flat, sloping or curved.

14 If you like, add a mosaic design to the fountain by pushing beads, buttons, sequins or small pebbles into the clay. Arrange them at random or create a pattern or colour scheme.

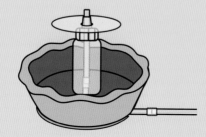

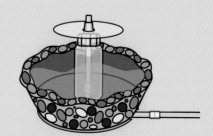

15 If you're using air-drying clay, wait for it to dry before using the fountain. You can now carefully move your fountain into position in your garden, with the water bottle nearby.

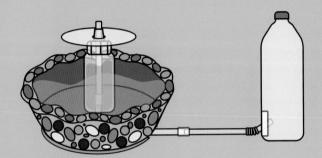

THE SCIENCE BIT!

Water can only flow from the bottle into the fountain when air can get in to replace it. When the lid is off, air pressure pushes the water down and out of the fountain. When the lid is on, the water stops flowing.

TIP

If you want the fountain to spout higher, leave the lid on, and squeeze the large bottle.

TAKE IT FURTHER ...

• Make lily pads to float in your fountain by cutting pad shapes out of green craft foam. You could make flowers from white and yellow foam, too.

• Use orange modelling clay to make some little goldfish!

FINISHING TOUCHES

Add the finishing touches to your garden with a fence to go around it, a path, seats and decorations. You can make all of these or just choose the ones you like.

First make sure everything you've made for your garden is arranged how you want it. If possible, leave spaces between different areas for paths and garden furniture.

FENCE AND GATE

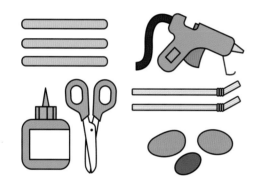

WHAT YOU NEED

- Lots of wooden craft sticks or lolly sticks
- Strong glue or a glue gun
- Scissors
- Two bendy straws
- Pebbles (optional)

1 To make a fence, arrange several sticks in a row. Glue two sticks across them at the top and bottom to hold them together.

2 Leave some space on the two vertical sticks at the edges, so that you can add more sections of fence and glue them together.

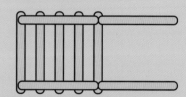

3 Stand sections of fence around the edges of the garden, just inside the tray. Use pebbles to hold the fence in place.

4 For a gate, make a separate section of fence. Cut off the long ends of the bendy straws. Glue the bendy sections to the fence and the gate to make bendy hinges.

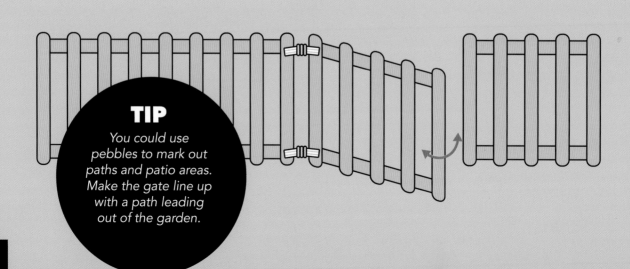

TIP

You could use pebbles to mark out paths and patio areas. Make the gate line up with a path leading out of the garden.

GARDEN FURNITURE

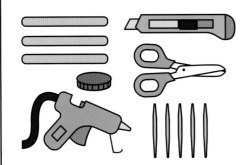

WHAT YOU NEED

- Wooden craft sticks
- Wooden cocktail sticks or skewers
- Strong scissors or craft knife
- Strong glue or a glue gun
- A plastic bottle lid (optional)

1 To make a seat, cut two short sections of wide craft stick about 3 cm long, using strong scissors or a craft knife.

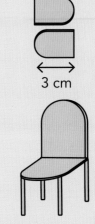

3 cm

2 Glue the pieces together in a seat shape. Stick pieces of thin craft sticks, wooden cocktail sticks or skewers, to the bottom to make legs.

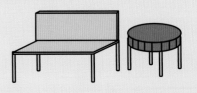

3 Try using larger pieces of craft stick to make benches or tables. You could make a round table from a plastic lid, with cocktail stick legs.

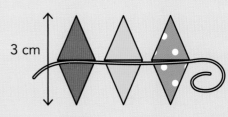

BUNTING

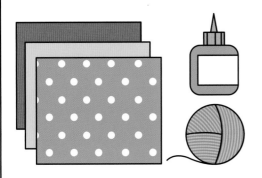

WHAT YOU NEED

- String or strong sewing thread
- Paper, felt or fabric scraps in different colours
- Glue

1 Cut lots of small diamond shapes, about 3 cm long, in different colours. Cut a piece of string the length you want your bunting.

3 cm

2 Fold the diamonds over the string to make triangles. Glue the two sides together.

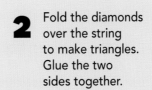

3 Tie the bunting between different parts of the garden, such as the summer house, greenhouse or fence.

AND HERE IS YOUR FINISHED GARDEN!

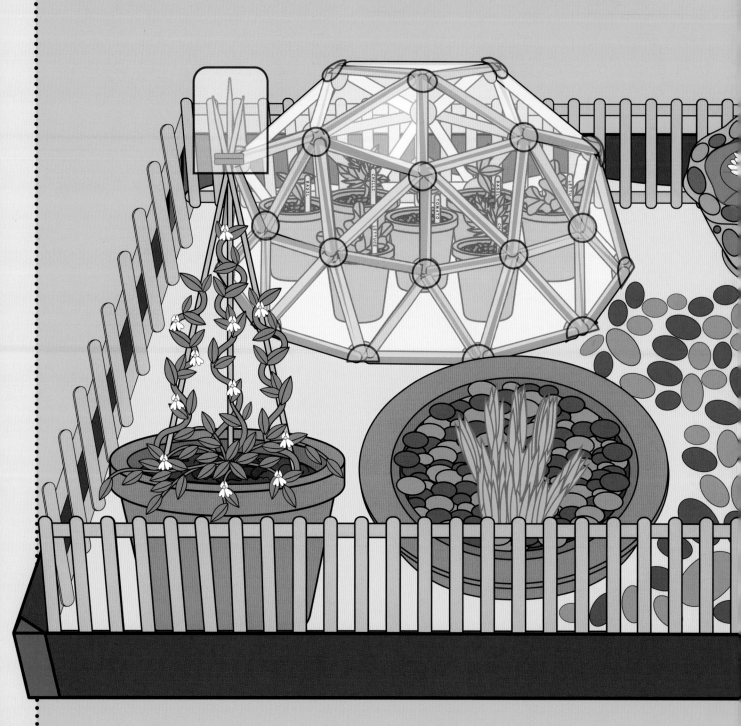